DEATH THRC
CLOCKWORK UNIVERSE

M000221617

DEATH THROES of the BROKEN CLOCKWORK UNIVERSE

Poems by
Wayne David Hubbard

atmosphere press

© 2022 Wayne David Hubbard

Cover design by Anonymous

Published by Atmosphere Press

No part of this book may be reproduced without permission from the author except in brief quotations and in reviews.

atmospherepress.com

DEDICATION

for the ones who made me sing

Teva,

May poetry guide you.

Thanks for your inspiration.

W. Duckett

PREFACE

This is my first poetry collection. For most of my life, I believed the purpose of life was to make sense of everything. Through poetry I have learned that life is for living, and, at times, making meaning from its boundless experiences.

These poems are portraits of where the poet has been. They cannot tell where the poet will go next. Such remains to be seen.

A few poems in this collection are like brown dwarfs -- objects in space existing as neither planets nor stars. They cannot become more, and yet, they refuse to yield. In these pages, their finality is accepted, and they are released.

All of these poems are survivors. The ones I carried... the ones that carried me.

Presented herein are observations of memory and place intertwined with my favorite themes: time, change, and love.

This is it.

~ W.D.H.

TABLE OF CONTENTS

PART ONE
The Time Studies

PART TWO
The Love Studies

PART ONE

The Time Studies

NIGHTWATCH

was it you
who told me

the capitols of the world
are burning?

i waited for you
until it was clear
that you would not come

how bright was our pleasure
how quickly we faded

yet in and in
we were perpetual

the blindness of dawn
the road at our feet

now that our assassins
have fallen asleep

MATRICES

I dreamt you returned all of my letters.
That night, a moon slid so close to the horizon
I thought we might walk across it.

An array is an ordered arrangement of elements,
Very unlike my memories of you.
So few, I admit
I multiplied us.

The next night, a dream unfolded in linear equations.
But the numerals vanished when I tried to solve.
All that remained were variables.

At daybreak,
One of us woke up whole.

EKPHRASTIC

animal presence. primal
presence. presence. presence.
eminence. fear. presence.
presence. presence. presence.
presence. presence. presence.
presence. presence. ferocity.
energy -- negativa.
gleaming
electric with life.

SPARKS
for Covid-19

like sparks flung from fire
some thousand miles away

one popped up
two came down
thanks to a little luck.

a man grabbed his book
the next day, he went to sea

to everyone's relief,
the story ended there.

IMMOBILIS

our god inside the tortoise shell
presiding over dark substance
a leader among the following
remains true to grace

FERNWEH

wanderlust is my middle name
unpenned verbs in the book of longing
alanis morissette crooning irony
through tinny speakers
at a bar in arizona

i raise a shot glass to you
and swallow it whole

CLASSIFIED

nightmare shadows day
tucked ring and necklace
under cross to assess
a willful blindness

QUIRANK

the country extends itself deep
it ebbs and flows beyond the quirank
which needs no description

but whether deep enough to salvage
the very excellent and good
we expect palpable conjecture

ASYLUM

a line to flood the asylum
they await their fates
as ridiculous as it sounds

LAMENTATION

War sullied our lungs.
How desperate were we
for the slightest crumb
of kindness?

Our hearts were wild;
our minds incendiary,
as we drank raw the violence.
At night, we slept in our tombs.

Soon the ghosts
will fill up this room,
and surround me in this room,

and what will become
of my memory of God?

PROOF of LIFE

After his nightly baptism
in secondhand smoke

He drove the speed limit
to buy baked bread.

Yet the real miracle came
when the light shone yellow

And he slowed
to a complete stop.

The REBELLION of SISYPHUS

at first
the stones
would not
speak to me

on my last push
they wept
that i would stay

only those
who chain death
can guess

how i reached
the other side

SOLUS

"...And when you gaze long into an abyss
the abyss also gazes into you."
 - Nietzsche, Beyond Good and Evil, Aphorism 146

this somnolent night

we sleep with doors open

when the void stares back

we do not stir

our body as solus

our shadow – the empire

our hopes – the color

of fire

COLUMBIA

capitol hill
rites of empire
suffering
   in stone

shaping
a consortium
   of one

beat
by beat
by beat

capitol fantasy
language for hire
and a little blue flag

still things
still lives
waiting to rise

unlike anything
ever seen before

HAIKUS

winter view (a)

spring bud slaked frozen
crystal floe of fog through night
at dawn, world of glass

winter view (b)

silver ice slivers
winter's metallurgic night
empyrean gem

winter view (c)

overwintered bud
dream time oscillations
a vernal hunger

winter view (d)

frozen ice droplet
clinging fast to window screen
space on either side

winter view (e)

cantered hourglass
snow like granular sugar
falling inside out

winter view (f)

derelict yule wreath
shattered ice sheaves on pavement
jaw of the blackbird

PROOF OF LIFE, NO. 3
for 2020

1.2.2021 – 77 Days to Spring

After the clamor year
  of proclamation and debate

Of giving until it hurts
  and hurts...

Profligacy,
  forgiveness,
    sobriety

Miles flown
  under night...

I prep myself for silence
  with knife and fork.

No decision
must be made
about bread.

Spring, summer, fall,
winter... spring
speak for the self
through a rosebush.

DEATH THROES of the BROKEN CLOCKWORK UNIVERSE

perennial cloud
that has no face
shriek of ages
song of me

days of rages
fires, mazes
concussive shudder
flash of me

inward fall
to the other sea
inside a ghost light
roar of me

nocturnal shroud
of that other eve
finite tremor
wisp of me

OPEN LETTER to
my HUNGRY NEIGHBOR NEXT DOOR

I, too, am almost from here
and wandered the labyrinth pitch
to find a gilded oasis

I, too, was almost worth
the wait

OPEN LETTER to the TYRANT GOD of MONSTERS

Never again shall my shadow blight
Thy halls of money and sadness

And, lo, would my soul be lifted clean,
Yea, carried unto the stars

May the earth not let go
 of my feet

OPEN LETTER to the
READER of THESE LETTERS

Continue, as you must,
On your road to the lustral city

Mind not
What becomes of me

I will find you there

IN a TIME LAPSE

1.

The fire burns low. I see your footsteps fading; your footprints
in sunken sand come to rest where I last belonged. If the glass of
water does not rattle across the table, it is not love. If there are no
pieces to reassemble; if a friend does not scramble to form a search
party for your sanity, it is not love. The fire burns low under-
ground. I read once of a woman who stood on her desk to
imagine swan-diving from fifteen stories into a wooden cup.
I awake and you are not here, yet neither am I; with neither
proof nor truth by which we can explain our exit from the time
lapse. Most days it is easier to be carried in the slipstream of daily
commitments; the detritus of someone else's purpose; a viper
flicking its tongue triumphantly tasting news of a meal to come.
I could sink my teeth into you; fall again, and again, and never
break free.

2.

I have made my journey through the time lapse.
Would you like to browse my elements?

Perchance my credentials as human being
could match your specific criteria?

There was a time I had loved and lost
which should be enough

but for sake of the advantage
allow me to continue.

There was a time
    I slammed my head into a wall.
        That was anger.

A time
    I waved goodbye as sunlight fell
    between canyon-like buildings.
        That was grief.

There was a scream
    that never reached my lips.

A cry that never reached heaven
    (nor would it be welcome).

A bone stretched across cinders
    waiting to be broken.

None of which appeals
    to daily jubilation.

But give me time,
    let one day I pass
        for human being

Before slipping quietly
    back into the time lapse.

3.

The hours elapse. Where did you go?
Your image in flickers continuously.

My core, layers deep,
iridescent, untouchable,
illuminating the uninhabitable.

They say now galaxies
hang like grape clusters
on invisible vines of dark matter.

Is this true?
Does Ra hold your hand?

Have you befriended Horus?
Have you made love to the dancing star?

4.

There were no victory marches. There were no defined borders.
There were no marked targets. There were no safe havens.

There were machines. There was blurred image.
There were innocent dead people.

There were conquerors of Alexandrian rites.
There were vicars of extermination and death.
They were warriors of the first order.

Be not fooled, vague pilgrim.
They roam the earth still among us.

There was a red moon before dawn,
but I slept through it.

There were meteors falling through Orion's belt...
    (for all life is poetry, where else should a meteor fall?)

The sun blights all:
I churn through daymares
like a housefly in a cup of water

All to gain seven six two
point zero zero American dollars.

I celebrate by wandering a museum.

5.

I had almost forfeited my birthright.
I had almost become a sovereign nation in my own right.
I had held you fully and known its truth.
I had almost made ready to let you go.
I had almost crowned you my muse
      for naming something is the first step of losing it.
I had forgotten to name myself.
I had brushed the face of a moon.
I had almost run out of faces.
I animated the ghost in the shell.

PART TWO

The Love Studies

THESE POEMS

these simple poems
these unadorned
natural words
  said plain
  and clear

these infinite games
this limitless song

these bright eyes
drinking you

ARIA, NO. 1

what i did is not
what i wanted
　　to do

it was as simple as this
　　i wished
　　to love you

so i built a thing
for the world
　　to see

and inscribed
your name
　　eternally

ARIA, NO. 2

we erected worlds
with our words

we made our moment
immortal and rich

what would it matter
if you knew my name?

i see you

ARIA, NO. 3

this landscape
touched only now
through dream

this room of peace
destroyed
by hurricane floods

those people
   (people, people everywhere)
   but not a core to eat

your arms about me
   (one last time)
   keeps me awake

our days like that
   i would yield

ARIA, NO. 4

you dream life
into truth

imagine me,
electric

in universe,
parallel

for you, my equal
appearing and new

i hold in my attitude
the favor of nations

i consume dark matter
and roar stars

ARIA, NO. 5

song of a thousand voices
merging in you

this flare streams
east–south–north
no flask can bare

three chords
in a single sphere

it is you

i perceive
imminent

ARIA, NO. 6

black shaped rude
comely reflection
emissary to life

look how bright
  we seared
    ourselves
      to canvas

which god will be
our drug tonight?

ARIA, NO. 7

what need have we
    of new days?

we – derelicts
    of now

what can tomorrow
    do for us?

bite this fruit

embrace
    no matter the cost

my name
    as it leaves
    your lung

most sweetbitter
    wound

this tongue

ARIA, NO. 8

light stars
    made up of

what else
    but us?

would i say
    i have found?

except

i was found
    by you

ARIA, NO. 9

the air you breathe
    becomes you

turn towards
    yourself

all that touches you
    yearns to feed you

look at how
loved you are

be embraced
    at last

ARIA, NO. 10

why courage in death
    and yet not life?

who will love for us
    once we are gone?

your search is done

my touch is here

we will be new

ARIA, NO. 11

but if i say,
i desire your freedom

have i not made
    a boundary
        of you?

the answer
    to life
        is yes

and now
the questions

DAY WATCH

The God of my lover
does not look for me

The God of my lover
is not the God of my soul

So much God talk
clouds the sky

In the city,
God builds her home
under a street lamp

In the country,
God sleeps
in the brushwood
where birds rest

Here,
even the light
has weight

Here,
even my God
has Gods

WORLD WITHOUT GYMNOPÉDIES

Her ache
a run-on sentence
beginning like,

Forgive me God,
for ever taking Satie
for granted

His song
a question
circling like,

What if language
cannot teach us
anything?

Play again
her childhood song
coming home like,

Memories bouyed
from sleep's pitched ink

Or joyful tears
blurring the notes
of sheet music

FUTURE PERFECT

I will have waited
many hours
  before seeing
  your face again

You will have found
some way to fill
  our absences

They will have not
believed us when we say
I love you

We will have known
  this all along

Which will have been
  enough

LOVE POEM for SAPPHO

when they ask
what it was like
we will say
we lived in a lighthouse
with nineteen million windows
and danced for the sea without a face
the gods will never believe
we fooled them into venerating us

HOW I MIGHT BE SPECTACULARLY WRONG

If I leave now, my changes will not be saved.
And if I stay, I may grow forgetful,
Like a fish in the sea, still thirsty.

If mercy mixed with turmeric and honey
Tastes something like cloud,

How will I know
When I have had enough to drink?

First I might imagine a slumbering bee,
Swathed in frozen night and clover dreams.

Next I could lose the proper question,
Moments before my turn to ask it.

Then a thought would bloom
Of how I might be spectacularly wrong

On the nature of flowers,
The mystery of nectar,

And other graces
Ever arriving ahead of me.

NOTES to a YOUNG POET

You are a kernel
Of an unrepeatable expression
In the history of a world.

Follow the dark star.

Between being awake and
Dreaming you are awake,
The diamonds are hidden.

Love will break you up
    through that concrete,
Leave you askance,
    yet priceless.

You are not fine wine.
You are not brass nor wood.
What you are -- money cannot buy.

Hide the center.
Give the rest away.

Be mindful of this:
Only the living are dying.

If they howl to scrape your bones,
Howl with them.

Go forward now,
No matter how you arrived,
Awaiting in vain that tepid rapture.

Interpretation is half the beauty.
The other half is you.

EQUITABLE DISTRIBUTION of LOVE
for Julie

we, the *intouchables*, go lightly

displacing baryons at will

deathless we dance

breathless we emerge

just as we are

ACKNOWLEDGMENTS

"Ekphrastic" : *Antediluvian*

"Love Poem for Sappho" : *Button Poetry*

"Aria, No. 7" and "Equitable Distribution of Love" :
The Wild Word

"The Rebellion of Sisyphus" : *Prometheus Dreaming*

"Notes to a Young Poet" and "Fernweh" :
The Dillydoun Review

"Columbia" and "Quirank" : *Eloquent Magazine*

"Proof of Life, No. 3" and "How I Might Be Spectacularly
Wrong" : *Shenandoah Valley Arts Council*

Other poems appear in this collection for the first time.

NOTES

The following poems were "found" from texts from newspaper articles and historic papers. Their content formed the baseline for each poetic work. Sources are listed in order of appearance.

Sparks

"Mapping the Path of the Virus from First U.S. Foothold" by Mike Baker. *The New York Times* | VOL. CLXIX. No. 58,671 | Wednesday, April 22, 2020.

Immobilis

"As They Honor King, Churches Ask: How Far Have We Come?" by John Eligon. *The New York Times* | Vol. CLXVII. No. 57,922 | Wednesday, April 4, 2018.

Classified

"Even Nightmares are Classified" by Sheri Fink. *The New York Times* | Vol. CLXVI. No. 57,415 | Sunday, November 13, 2016.

Quirank

According to English Colonial Papers (1607), Quirank is the Powhatan name given to the present-day Blue Ridge Mountains of Virginia and West Virginia. This information was republished in *The Virginia Historical Magazine* (1906), Vol. I, 151., page 374.

Asylum

"Trump Returns To a Hard Line On Immigrants" by Julie Hirschfeld Davis. *The New York Times* | Vol. CLXVII. No. 57,921 | Tuesday, April 3, 2018.

ABOUT the AUTHOR

Wayne David Hubbard is the author of *Mobius: Meditations on Home*, and his poems and essays have appeared in *Button Poetry, The Good Men Project,* and various literary journals. Born and raised in New Jersey, he now lives in Virginia and works in aviation. Learn more at <u>waynedavidhubbard.com</u>.

CPSIA information can be obtained
at www.ICGtesting.com
Printed in the USA
BVHW042306260922
648046BV00002B/101

9 781639 884759